COUNTRY LIVING
Easy Makeovers
101 Quick Design Fixes
You Can Do in a Weekend

COUNTRY LIVING

Easy Makeovers

101 Quick Design Fixes You Can Do in a Weekend

MICHELE KEITH

HEARST BOOKS
A division of Sterling Publishing Co., Inc.

New York / London
www.sterlingpublishing.com

Copyright © 2008 by Hearst Communications, Inc.

Library of Congress Cataloging-in-Publication Data
Keith, Michele.
   Country living easy makeovers : 101 quick design fixes you can do in a
weekend / Michele Keith.
       p. cm.
   Includes index.
   ISBN 978-1-58816-659-3
1. Interior decoration—Handbooks, manuals, etc. I. Country living (New
York, N.Y.) II. Title. III. Title: Easy makeovers. IV. Title: 101 quick design fixes
you can do in a weekend.
   NK2115.K36 2007
   747—DC22
           2007007612

10 9 8 7 6 5 4 3 2 1

Published by Hearst Books
A Division of Sterling Publishing Co., Inc.
387 Park Avenue South, New York, NY 10016

Country Living and Hearst Books are trademarks of
Hearst Communications, Inc.
www.countryliving.com

For information about custom editions, special sales, premium and
corporate purchases, please contact Sterling Special Sales Department at
800-805-5489 or specialsales@sterlingpub.com.

Distributed in Canada by Sterling Publishing
c/o Canadian Manda Group, 165 Dufferin Street
Toronto, Ontario, Canada M6K 3H6

Distributed in Australia by Capricorn Link (Australia) Pty. Ltd.
P.O. Box 704, Windsor, NSW 2756 Australia

Manufactured in China

Book design by Anna Christian

Sterling ISBN 978-1-58816-659-3

FOREWORD

Is there ever enough time to make the house exactly as we want it? No. But with foresight and planning, there are hundreds of things that can be done over the course of a weekend that will not only make it look different and better, and give it real country flair, but allow it to truly reflect the style and personality of you and your family.

Dreaming of something too ambitious for a single weekend? Break it into two or three segments and enjoy the satisfaction of completing each. All thumbs? Don't worry. The 101 tips we've gathered in this book were designed with you in mind. Easy to do? Definitely. Professional, high-quality results? Absolutely.

We recommend making your "weekend makeover" fun, as well as simple and fast, by getting your spouse or a good friend to help. An extra set of eyes and hands is always helpful.

So now that you know it's possible, it's time to create a plan. Flip through this book, which is arranged in sections dedicated to specific areas of decorating, and decide what best suits your needs: walls, floors, furniture, window treatments, accessories, or collections ... or a few of each. Some of the ideas can be used in any room of the house; others are room specific, better suited to living or dining room, bedroom, kitchen, or bath. We've also included tips on finding, measuring, and maintaining, so that regardless of what you choose to do, it will be as easy as possible to get it right the first time— and to keep it looking great for years to come.

Happy decorating!

Nancy Mernit Soriano
Editor-in-Chief, *Country Living*

CHAPTER ONE

THE THRILL
OF
THE HUNT

✳

The Wheres and Hows of Finding Good Stuff

One great flea-market find can transform a room in no time.
Whether you want to start or add to a collection, or seek that
perfect piece that will become a decorating focal point,
here are tips for how to find what you're looking for—along with
creative ideas for putting unexpected treasures to use.

1

Keep your eyes open. Great finds are everywhere. In addition to Web sites, remember to search out salvage companies (they're especially good for bathroom fixtures, tubs and sinks, mantelpieces, and architectural elements), the Salvation Army, Goodwill, mail-order outlets, thrift and second-hand shops, swap meets, garage sales, brick-and-mortar and online outlet stores, church fairs, street fairs, flea markets, town dumps, and sidewalks (if custom dictates leaving things out for others to pick up). Also useful are remodeling and demolition firms that might have items scrapped from old buildings that you can use.

> **“** My best source for something special is eBay. It's great for china, glassware, flatware, as well as one-of-a-kind pieces. Be very specific when entering a name in the search engine. You'll be pleasantly surprised with what pops up. **”**

Nicole Esposito Polly
Country Living contributing editor

2

Take your time. Searching is part

of the fun. You'll be happiest with pieces that "speak" to you, touching your heart, as well as being a bargain. Look for items that you and your family can actually use, as well as admire. When you see "it," you'll know it.

3

Ask questions.

Reputable dealers expect this and are happy to provide the answers: "Do you have the other one of this pair? Where is this from? Will polishing/cleaning improve its appearance? What can you tell me about these markings?" Don't be shy; if items are not labeled with price tags, ask the seller: "How much?" You may also ask: "Can you do better with the price?" Do, however, keep in mind that if the sign says, "prices firm" or words to that effect, you should respect it.

4

Plan ahead for a day of flea-marketing.

Think about how you want your house to look and feel, and the types of things that might create that effect. Bring photos of the rooms you're focusing on, or a digital camera with the photos you've taken in it, and notes you've made regarding the dimensions of the rooms and the pieces you're looking for (length, width, height, and depth) when going out to "hunt." Bring along a notepad and pen to jot down locations of items you see but want to think about before returning to buy, and for noting names and phone numbers of dealers who specialize in what pleases you.

Bring cash for those who do not accept checks or credit cards. Remember that prices may be lowered in the late afternoon or if you buy more than one item from a vendor, so wear comfy shoes and be ready for a long day.

APPRAISAL OVERVIEW

1. **Find an appraiser** through such reputable organizations as:

* **Appraisers Association of America:** www.appraisersassoc.org (212.889.5404)

* **American Society of Appraisers:** www.appraisers.org (703.478.2228)

* **International Society of Appraisers:** www.isa-appraisers.org (206.241.0359)

2. **Average fee for a written appraisal** is $100–$300 per hour

3. **Provide as much material and information** as possible:

* Previous appraisal documents

* Original receipts

* Photographs

* Historical documentation

* Restoration reports

5

Shop smart. Even if it's only $1, if the item you're considering ends up being useless, it's $1 that could have gone to something wonderful. When an item catches your eye, judge its condition: Sit on it, open and close it, turn it upside down and all around. Ask what it's made of if it isn't evident, so that you can determine if you have the time and patience to care for it correctly. Check for dry rot, termites, and wobbly legs and arms. If you have children at home, be careful of old finds with flaking paint that can be dangerous if ingested. And lastly, if chunks of wood or embellishments are missing, think about the cost of replacement or consider if you can use it as is and be happy.

6

Reassign to a new use.

A piano bench or flat topped trunk can make a terrific coffee table; a church pew can make great seating in your home; old linens, sheets, rolls of fabric, and lightweight bedspreads can be fabulous coverings for pillows or turned into curtains; architectural elements like corbels, plinths, finials, and brackets add character and style to shelves and windows; tote bags holding office supplies, magazines, or mittens and hats can look super hung on the wall; toy chests can hold towels and cleaning supplies in the bathroom, as well as provide seating; vintage silver toast racks are a beautiful and unusual means for holding mail and take-out menus; buffets can be turned into vanities; old towel racks will add a hint of the past to your cottage-style kitchen; medicine cabinets make great shelving (minus their doors); ice buckets with pebbles placed on the bottom for drainage make divine planters; a curly iron gate can form a lyrical composition on a wall that's as brilliant as an Old Master painting—or be transformed into a pot rack in the kitchen; fireplace mantels become sculpture when hung on a wall, with or without the addition of a mirror in the open space. The possibilities are endless.

7

Bad can be beautiful.
Pieces that have faults can often be transformed into useful and good-looking finds. For example, an end table whose top has seen better days can look terrific with a tray of the right size set upon it; an entry-hall table can be your new coffee table simply by cutting its long legs down to size; and a tired old chest of drawers might enjoy new life in the kid's room with a splash of bright paint.

8

Get framed. Scour flea markets and garage sales for
old picture frames in different shapes, sizes, and materials. With
wood frames, if you like the look as is, whether elegantly smooth
or delightfully chipped and battered, just dust off. If the wood is
not your taste, paint it. White is always good for patterned walls,
whereas gold is a knockout against deep blues, reds, and greens.
Determine the best arrangement for multiple frames by
experimenting on a table or the floor before hanging to avoid
misplaced nail holes.

9

A word to the wise. The Internet can be
a marvelous resource for fabulous finds, but with it
comes the need for caution. Usually, you're not buying
from the site itself, so it won't accept responsibility if
things go wrong with the goods you purchase. Check
terms and conditions from all the people/Web sites from
which you buy. Some online businesses have ratings
posted by past purchasers, which can be useful.
Regardless of your purchase, keep in mind that colors
will always differ to a certain degree from what you see
on your monitor.

Among the most common problems are:

* Goods not delivered to buyer

* Goods arrive damaged from shipping

* Goods of lesser value or differing from posted
  description sent to buyer

* Late delivery of goods

* Failure to provide relevant information about
  product/terms of sale

BUYING ONLINE

* **Before purchasing an item,** question the seller about authenticity, condition, and provenance. There are also online companies that provide such advice.

* **Learn how to bid and buy online** in classes held across the country through eBay University. Visit ebay.com/university for details.

* **Resist paying too much**—there will always be more auctions and different items to be found tomorrow.

* **If you're bidding on something you really want,** stay on top of the auction's progress until the very end, as last-minute bids are common. Remember: Most auctions finish on Pacific Standard Time.

* **If the price is right, take a risk.** Chances are you'll be pleasantly surprised.

* **Don't skimp on shipping insurance**—especially if item is breakable or costly.

CHAPTER TWO

SURROUND YOURSELF WITH BEAUTY

✳

What to Do with the Walls

With a single can of paint, you can become a quick-change artist. Nothing freshens up a room like a new coat of paint—choose a lighter palette to brighten the walls, or a deeper shade for a dramatic look, paint a single room detail, or even just the trim. In the mood for greater texture? Wallpaper's a snap. Like your walls as they are, but looking to embellish the ambience? Read on for ideas on creative displays.

10

Rev up with paint. Of course you'll want to consider the walls, but don't forget the trim—window and door molding, fireplace mantel and surround, doors, wainscoting, or paneling. You might paint one of these areas or several. You could even do something special with the ceiling. The possibilities are vast:

* Repeat the dominant color in the room's décor.

* Paint trim a lighter or darker shade of the wall color.

* Paint trim a color on the opposite side of the color wheel from the wall color.

* Paint only one architectural feature that you want to bring attention to, such as French doors, a fireplace, or an interestingly shaped window.

* Pick up a color that you've used sparingly, but adore— perhaps from the sofa pillows or a pair of candlesticks.

* Use white for trim if everything else is a color.

11

Tell a story. Cover massive areas of wall space with framed photos or paper ephemera that tells a story. Choose pieces that are meaningful to you—vacations, family portraits, landscapes you love, or colorful restaurant menus—and let them weave a narrative as viewers move from left to right, top to bottom, past large and small images.

12

Use the best paint for the job. Keep in mind that *matte* works well for most ceilings and walls because its flat finish does not accentuate surface irregularities, while *satin* has a gentle sheen that lends a soothing glow to a bedroom, bath, or study. Also, satin paint can be cleaned.

Light, warm tones of any color family are generally easier to live with than dark, cool shades. If you want the snap of a bright color, it's usually best to save it for small areas, furniture, and accessories.

> *" Painting the floorboards white is a relatively inexpensive way to make a house look fresh and up-to-date without requiring that you decorate from top to bottom. "*
>
> Cath Kidston, British textile and accessories designer

Texture is another feature to consider; it adds a nice touch of extra oomph. There are paints with suede, stucco, and sand finishes built right in, but if you can't find what you want, look for texturizing agents that can be added to the paint.

A third option that's as easy as can be is to create a textured appearance by combing, sponging, or ragging the paint as you go. An extra bonus these processes offer is that besides providing a great-looking finish, they cover flaws, such as uneven surfaces, bumps, and cracks.

13

Be subtle with the ceiling. If you're unsure about painting it a strong color, begin gradually. Add some of the wall color to a gallon of white paint. The ceiling will seem less stark, flow better with the walls, and yet remain understated. Or choose a tint of a contrasting color already in your palette.

14

Do a color check. Color is greatly affected by light. To be sure you'll like your choice 24/7, make a test run. Buy a pint-size can of the paint you're thinking about and paint a foot-square piece of white paper. Hang it where you plan to paint. Look at it at different times of the day and night—all the times you will be using the room, with lights on and off. Your color choices might be absolutely perfect, or you may decide to try a lighter or darker shade—or something totally different.

EASY PAINTING

* **Determine amount of paint needed:** Find the number of square feet (multiply each wall's height by its width). One gallon of smooth paint covers up to approximately 350 square feet, while one gallon of textured paint covers roughly 300 square feet.

* **Prep the area:** Remove furniture, curtains, and knick-knacks that might get in the way; dust the area to be painted; patch up any cracks or holes; mask areas you don't want to paint, such as window moldings and base-boards, with blue painter's tape. Lay a drop cloth on the floor. Keep rags handy for drips. Wear rubber gloves that are thin enough to allow a comfortable grasp on the brush or roller, yet thick enough to keep hands paint-free.

* **Use high-quality brushes and rollers:** Ask store personnel to help you select the correct kinds of bristles and shapes for each particular job. Before buying, tug at the bristles. If more than two come out, don't buy it.

* **Allow time to dry:** When finished, carefully peel off all tape and allow the surfaces to dry completely.

* **Ventilate properly:** Whether it's paint or primer, be sure the room you're working in has fans, open windows, or other sources of ventilation.

15

Brighten a small area with paint.

Consider the often overlooked places that you could jazz up with a few brush strokes: In many homes, the pass-through between living room and kitchen gets lots of use, so why not make the most of it? Choose a color that complements the counter, be it butcher block, tile, or stone. Or perhaps the door of your pantry could use a refresher. Pick a bright color. It'll go great with all the goodies inside. Or why not paint the interior of the bar area or bookshelves, including the walls within them? Whether one shade or several, when completed, the entire area will look like a piece of art, and set off books and knickknacks to best advantage.

"We're obsessed with color. It's the joy of life. Many people like to begin with walls. Do the trim in white. If you have no moldings, paint one wall a strong color—red or cobalt blue. This will make the room appear bigger while adding style and depth."

Anthony Baratta and William Diamond, interior designers

16

Trim with flowers. Buy dried flowering vines (such as hops) or dry them yourself. Then tack them to the walls like molding, to frame mirrors and tops of doorways. They add a homey, rustic touch and because their colors are so muted as to be nearly neutral, they'll blend with almost any decorating style.

17

Repurpose favorite textiles. If you have a colorful quilt or nicely patterned tablecloth that spends more time folded up in a trunk than out in the open for all to see and admire, use it as wall art. Hang it from a wooden dowel or curtain rod that is sturdy and in correct proportion to the textile's weight and size. You could do the same thing with a large piece of pretty fabric. If the piece echoes the colors or complements the patterns of the furniture or carpet, it can pull an entire room together in a fresh, new way.

18

Add magic to a child's room. Paint silver stars and moons over walls and ceiling, or arch a rainbow over the bed's headboard. Clouds are another clever choice—especially if the walls are already pastel blue, as are flowers, grass, and trees that "sprout" from the baseboards, with a sun shining above. Doing any of these would be a fun project for the whole family.

19

Make history with ready-made materials.

If you are handy with a saw, hammer, and nails, one of the most effective ways to dress up walls is to add store-bought decorative molding. Once affixed and stained or painted, it looks as though it's been a part of the house for 100 years.

Among the many types are *crown molding*—for use along the wall at ceiling level; *architrave* or *door headers* put above doors; *fluted molding*—often used at either side of a door or fireplace; *casings*—used around doors and windows; *chair rails*—installed anywhere from 24" to 48" from the floor; *plinth blocks*—squares of wood put where the baseboard meets the casing at the door's edges; *panel molding*—a square of wood used as a decorative element for walls; *wainscot paneling*—trim put below chair rails; *corner guards*—used where walls come together; and *baseboard*—placed along the wall at the floor.

One can also find *medallions* to embellish ceiling-mounted light fixtures and *corbels* that hold up shelves and mantels or just look like they do. The variety of styles and woods available are vast; many are also made in such materials as resin and polyurethane. But remember: One or two of these are usually all you need to make a huge difference.

20

Add a splash of color.

Paint a color on one wall in an all-white room to act as a frame for the furniture in front of it, reinforce the dominant color of a patterned carpet for a more cohesive look, or add interest to an otherwise boring, white box of a room. It's simple to create contrasting stripes or a large block of plaid on one wall—block them out with masking tape to ensure straight edges.

21

Try paint that is practical and fun.

Chalkboard paint is fun in a child's room, or on a door in the kitchen, basement, or wherever family members stop before heading out. Just as in the classrooms of the 1940s and '50s, its finish is perfect for drawing on and doing homework, and posting reminders about dental appointments and what to pick up at the grocery store.

22

Create architectural interest
with paint.
Many homes built today lack the charming details that make older homes so unique and desirable. But with the magic of paint, you can give even a sleek city apartment the feel of a rustic farmhouse. Follow classic examples with the colors that go with your room. You can paint faux chair rails, crown moldings, and baseboards, or even paint a frieze.

23

Stenciling is nearly foolproof.

Limited only by your imagination, you can buy stencils and rubber stamps with all sorts of beautiful designs in an array of sizes. A stencil brush and cream-formula stencil paints that are less prone to drip than wall paint will help to ensure successful results. It's a good idea to mark the walls where you want to begin and end, and to practice your painting skills on a piece of paper before attacking the wall.

Go for a Dutch farmhouse look by stenciling a border close to the ceiling and repeating it around window and door frames. For more elegance, cover an entire wall with a large-scale stencil, perhaps medallions or flowers. One small graphic design applied in a regular pattern can be as chic as any silk wall covering. A third choice is to create fake panels using readymade molding and then fill them with a stenciled pattern.

24

Make wallpaper art. If you're really enamored with wallpaper and want to be exceptionally original without doing the entire room, create a collage with squares of different papers—ask design stores for books of discontinued wallpapers, or pick up vintage rolls at the flea market. A unique way to highlight one wall in a room is to pin up the squares you've cut into the size you want, and arrange them until you're happy with the overall look. Then draw chalk outlines on the wall to ensure even, professional-looking results. Begin pasting the squares in the center, overlapping the edges as you work your way out. For fun, use newspaper instead of wallpaper in a closet, powder room, or other small space.

E A S Y
W A L L P A P E R I N G

* **Determine number of rolls of wallpaper needed per wall:** Find the square footage to be covered (multiply the total width of the wall by its height) and divide by the square footage in one roll of the wallpaper you are considering; depending on manufacturer, wallpaper yields vary from 27 to 33 square feet per roll.

* **Prep the surface:** Take down the old paper; remove any loose plaster; fill holes and cracks; and then sand any rough spots.

* **Cover the area with primer and sizing,** which will allow easier positioning of wallpaper.

* **Mark plumb lines for use as a guide:** Starting at one corner, measure the width of the paper minus half an inch. Draw a vertical line with pencil or chalk using a spirit level or plumb bob.

* **Affix to wall:** For a smooth finish, abut edges of each new strip of wallpaper up against the edge of the strip already glued into place rather than overlapping the seams.

25

Revitalize with wallpaper. It can change

proportions, make a ceiling seem higher, produce a more intimate
feeling in a large space, or dramatize a room's best features, but if
you find hanging wallpaper a bit intimidating, you can always
save it for just one wall or a small space, like the sloping wall under
the eaves in the sewing room, the area surrounding the medicine
cabinet in the bathroom, or the wall behind a sofa or bed.

26

If it's beautiful, consider it art.

Mount interesting window frames (think arched ones from old churches), iron gates, garden trellises, columns, or tall shutters on a bare wall. Their texture and shape will provide a sense of history, as well as decoration for the room. Check for items like these in architectural salvage stores if you don't come across them in your regular haunts. Display them as you find them, nicked and battered, or refresh them with a coat of paint. If you're concerned about the amount of weight the wall can bear, or your ability to put up a heavy object, lean it against the wall. It might look just as good—maybe even better.

CHAPTER THREE

FROM THE BOTTOM UP

Fabulous Floors

The floor is the anchor of any design scheme, and making a change to it is a quick way to add warmth, texture, color, or an extra graphic element to a room. Whether you choose carpets and rugs, paint, wood, or ceramic tile, you have the world at your feet when it comes to decorative options.

27

Check it. For kitchen or bath, create a checkerboard floor with self-stick vinyl tiles. Inexpensive and available in a range of colors and sizes, they are easy to apply. Try ideas out first with construction paper in the colors and sizes you have in mind. Lay them out to verify proportion, scale, and harmony. Prepare the floor by removing the previous floor covering, pulling out loose or protruding nails, and sanding the sub-floor. Work in quadrants from the center of the room outward. Trim the tiles to fit along the outer edges.

28

Paint your wood floor. Painted patterns,

such as big diamonds in contrasting colors or a black-and-white checkerboard—large or small, are beautiful enhancements that let you use your floor to its best advantage. You could also stencil it with motifs from a kit or add your own freehand design. Depending upon the condition of the wood, some prep work

might be required first. While checks and stripes are easy, complex patterns benefit from a sure eye—for them the trick is for one color to dominate and for all hues to be within the overall scheme used in the room.

Directions:

* **Decide on a design.** Sketch it out and play with the proportions.

* **Sand and prime**, then paint the entire floor with the lighter color of the design, using interior latex paint in a flat finish.

* **Draw it onto the floor** if the pattern is geometric. Use water-soluble colored pencils and a ruler, then isolate specific areas with painter's tape. Using appropriate size rollers, apply the second paint color in your pattern. If using stencils, mark guides for the stencil placement and then apply the paint with a stencil brush. Let the paint dry; then repeat with each color desired.

* **Finish with sealant** (a few coats to protect the floor) and add gloss.

29
Decorate your rugs.

Glue-gun or tack a fabric band around the
perimeter of a small area rug, perhaps a solid-
colored suede around sisal or velvet around
needlepoint. Widths will vary depending upon
the look desired or the need to conceal wear-
and-tear. This simple addition can make an
inexpensive rug look luxe, give a formal rug
a more casual air, or an informal one a dressier
look, and extend the life of one that is worn.

30

Install a carpet on your stairs.

There are two popular stair carpet styles: Waterfall, where the carpet flows continuously down the stairs, tacked at regular intervals for security; and New York, with carpet-covered treads and bare risers. The carpet needn't match any rug you have nearby, but should complement it. You could also paint or stencil the risers a color or design that goes well with the walls and treads.

" Throughout history, rugs have been the glory of decorating. **"**

Billy Baldwin, renowned interior decorator of the 1950s

31

Embellish the floor. Consider decoupaging
a wallpaper border on your floor. Carefully glue the paper to
the floor, and smooth out wrinkles. When it's firmly in place,
apply two coats of water-based polyurethane as a protective
sealant over it and the entire floor.

32

Make a rug. Gather self-adhesive carpet tiles in colors that harmonize with your furnishings. Create a solid, a pattern with contrasting border, or your own unique design. For a cozy look, choose carpet tiles with a deep plush or chunky woven surface.

33

Try small rugs. Big problems like dingy
wall-to-wall carpeting, stained hardwood, or scuffed-up
linoleum can be hidden with small, carefully placed rugs.
They can also add a light touch for summer or warm up
a room in winter. Tiny patterned rugs, even remnants,
add a cozy feel when placed in such unexpected places
as before a bureau, under a bench at the foot of a bed, or
in front of the kitchen sink. And don't be afraid to put
several in one room. As long as they have a common
aspect of color or design, they'll look great together.

34

Stain it. Instead of paint or a traditional wood shade of stain, try a color—maybe even two or three shades of it. Cover imperfect flooring of any shade: To create light, medium, and dark tones, simply use one, two, or three coats of the same stain. Be sure the floor is free of wax and grease before beginning. If creating a pattern, mask the floor with tape before you start; if following the floorboards to create stripes, mark the baseboards to indicate which floorboards to stain which color as it's easy to get confused. Apply a coat of polyurethane varnish once all the stain is dry.

35

Layer rugs for winter. If you
like a cozy look for the cold months, but have
no place to put your summer sisal rug if you
remove it, simply put another rug on top of it.
Topped with a richly patterned Persian, old-
fashioned needlepoint, or a braided rug picked
up at a county fair, it will make the entire room
feel winterized.

36

Remove rugs. It's a natural thing to do when warm weather comes, but can be done any time of the year. A buffed and polished wood floor instead of carpeting will change the mood and feeling of any room—rolling up the rugs is faster than nearly anything else you can do.

CHAPTER FOUR

FABULOUS FURNISHINGS

✳

*Fresh Takes and Fix-ups
for Furniture*

One great piece can change the focus of a room.
Furniture you love but have grown tired of can find a new
life in another room, perhaps taking on a decidedly different
purpose. Give it a new color, add some bright cushions,
drape it with a luxurious throw—you've changed the look
and mood of a room in an instant.

"When you mix a few good pieces with non-pedigreed items, it raises the level of everything."

Randy Florke
Country Living
Contributing Editor

37

Repurpose furniture.

Try an upholstered pouf topped with a big sturdy tray as a coffee table—two hassocks placed side-by-side work for this too. Use a metal file cabinet, no longer needed in the office, to hold supplies in the laundry room or nails and tools in the basement. Take a chair from the garden, make a terrycloth-covered pillow for it, and put it in the bathroom for a spa-like touch.

Turn a collection of vintage suitcases into a novel side table or stack books on an extra chair for use as a bedside nightstand—top with a lamp and clock radio. If you're handy, wire the interior of a step-back cupboard for lights, and transform it into a bar filled with glasses and your favorite beverages, nuts and bowls, cocktail stirrers, and napkins. Or skip the wiring, and simply paint the interior bright red or gold.

38

Mix it up. For a fresh take in the dining or breakfast room, forego chairs that match the table; instead, use garden-variety wooden or metal styles, adding cushions if needed. Or bring out a similarly bold spirit by painting classic Victorian or Queen Anne chairs a hot pink or cobalt blue or covering their seat cushions with a contemporary, printed fabric—of course, don't paint anything that has value as an antique.

39

Spruce up chairs. Sew a quick-and-easy mini-cover for your ladder-back chair. All you need is a rectangular length of fabric. Fold it wrong-side out to form a pocket, stitch the two sides closed, hem the open edge, and then turn it right side out. Add a big, ornamental button or fabric nosegay to one side, or embroider your initials for extra pizzazz.

40

Add a jolt of color. Energize a room or hallway done up in a single palette by adding a few accessories in a contrasting hue. Not only will it enliven the space, it will strengthen and accentuate the basic design scheme.

41

Transform with paint.

If the chairs ringing your breakfast table are different shapes or styles, create a newly harmonious look by painting them all the same color. Conversely, if they're identical in appearance, paint each a different shade.

For a bureau, try painting stripes or creating a plaid on the drawers, leaving the rest of the piece a solid color that coordinates.

An especially nice touch for a child's room would be a poem painted on a chest, a different line on each drawer. Easiest of all, paint knobs a color that contrasts with the drawers, or make freehand stars and moons over the entire piece.

FURNITURE PAINTING SMARTS

* **Before painting,** fill dents and holes with wood filler and let dry.

* **Lightly sand** the entire piece and wipe clean.

* **Paint** with a water-based primer; let dry.

* **Follow with a base coat** of latex paint and let dry.

* **Apply designs** freehand or use stencils or stamps. Let dry.

* **Protect** with two coats of clear, water-based polyurethane, letting dry thoroughly between coats.

42

Paint the tub. Add a splash of color to the bathroom by painting the exterior of your cast-iron tub. (If you don't have one, there are plenty of salvage companies that do!) First, thoroughly clean it, then apply latex primer with a foam roller and let it dry to create a smooth surface. Paint at least two coats of exterior-grade latex paint in a satin or semi-gloss finish with a foam roller. Silver leaf (faux is fine) is an alternative that is both Victorian and very elegant.

If you wish, go a step further: Personalize it with a stenciled or freehand design with latex or an oil-based paint. The motif could reflect or contrast with the window or shower curtains, or mirror the look of the countertop or floor. When cleaning, avoid products with gritty agents that could damage your artistry.

43

Cover with a copy. There's lots more than paint that can disguise an old file cabinet, table, or anything else with a flat surface. Photocopy a favorite image from a poster, wallpaper, or fabric, and enlarge or miniaturize to suit. Affix with rubber cement or decoupage medium-size pieces, overlapping the edges as you go, and carefully smooth out the wrinkles. Paint on a layer of clear sealant to protect from wear and tear.

44

Store books in interesting ways.

Stack books on an old wooden bench or side chairs.
In a child's room, use a toy ironing board or little red
wagon. For any room of the house, antique plate
racks will add charm as well as keep books handy
and neatly organized.

> " Country style is all about relaxed, comfortable, and causal living. I love to mix antiques with new fabrics to create a look both rustic and elegant. "
>
> Sheila Bridges, interior designer, author of *Furnishing Forward*

45

Move it around. There's no law that says furniture must stay in the room it was designed for. Try putting a twin bed (four-posters without canopies, campaign-style ones with decorative heads and feet, and mattress-and-box-spring beds work best) in the living room in place of an ordinary sofa. Dressed up with a decidedly non-bedroom-style throw, no one will ever guess where you got it. Other relocation candidates include a child's desk or small, antique writing table to use as a vanity in the bathroom, or a hammock hung in the family room for extra seating.

46

Divide and conquer.

A bookcase is a natural room divider, and a handy one, especially if it has no back so that shelves filled with knickknacks, candlesticks, photos, and books can complement both spaces. If there's room between its top and the ceiling, add some silk plants or topiaries. Make sure the case is steady, securing it to ceiling or floor if need be.

If you don't have any extra bookcases on hand, seek out one or two (real or fake) columns at the flea market or salvage shop. The beauty of these architectural elements is that while they give the illusion of a break in the floor plan, there is nothing that "stops" the eye, thus preserving a feeling of spaciousness. Tall and short ones work equally well.

47

Toss on color and pattern.

Rather than buying slipcovers for your furniture, find shawls, throws, quilts, afghans, or baby blankets to toss over sofa backs and arms, hassocks, and chairs. Fold into rectangles or triangles, or cover the entire back or seat with them, tucking them into the crevices to keep them neat. Adding color and texture, these additions tie color schemes together, and can bring an intimate, ethnic, or elegant warmth to the entire room. Showy shawls and runners are classic enhancements for pianos, sideboards, and side tables too.

48

Match cabinet exteriors to interiors.

Paint the glass doors of a cabinet to look like whatever you store in it; go for a stylized effect if fine art is not your forte. Paint the interior side of the panes, using the "reverse" painting technique—meaning you apply the foremost portion of the design first and then paint the background over it. When the layers of your design are dry, apply a coat of a dark shade to give the panel interiors a contrasting appearance when the doors are open. Paint the wood inside and out a complementary color.

49

Make your bed. So many things can be turned into a headboard that you'll want to change yours seasonally. In addition to such possibilities as covering the existing headboard with fabric, a coverlet, or small rug, you could create a new one for a simple mattress-and-box-spring set with an old barn door placed horizontally, or if the bed is wide, two of them positioned vertically, to bring an architectural element into the room. Iron or wood garden gates, mailbox posts, and white picket fences are other whimsical headboard options. Nearly any style of fireplace mantel will look great, especially if after securing it to the wall, you cover the opening with fabric. Its ledge makes the perfect spot for candlesticks, books, and family photos. Another simple idea is a curtain rod positioned squarely over the bed and hung with draperies.

50

Reinvent beds.
Soften the sleek lines of a contemporary four-poster bed by hanging fabric or a curtain from the rod above the bed head. Or create a wavy canopy overhead by floating a length of organza from front to back, allowing the middle to swag a bit and the end to flutter halfway to the floor. The same system is equally effective with a heavy material like duck or ticking—remember both sides will show so you might want to line these if they are patterned.

CHAPTER FIVE

LET THE SUNSHINE IN... OR KEEP IT OUT

✳

Wonderful Window Treatments

Window treatments frame the natural light and form a backdrop
for your furnishings, and most are as easy as 1, 2, 3 to change
with the season or your whims. Whether you purchase them,
sew them, toss up no-sew options, or embellish existing,
go for fabric that creates the ambiance you crave.

51

Dress up the windows.

While naked windows are perfect for certain rooms, sometimes it's necessary to filter incoming light, create a sense of privacy, cover up an unpleasant view, or simply make the interiors look more "finished." While readymade options abound, two of the easiest styles to make are a simple ruffle or valance to hang at the top and café curtains that cover the bottom half. In both cases, to make a casing for the rod, simply fold the fabric 1 to 2 inches over along the top, then sew or glue in place. Or purchase café clips and skip the casing. Be sure to hem, bind, or pink the edges for a finished look.

52

Brighten bare windows. Four easy options: Hang a small mirror on a velvet ribbon or invisible fishing line; rest a small-framed painting or two atop the sash; line up potted plants, autumn squash, or decorative pitchers on the windowsill; or create a cascade of crystal prisms in different shapes and sizes by tying them onto ribbons secured with a bow at the top.

53

Pair curtains and blinds. A foolproof way to give windows dressed with curtains or blinds a new look is to add whichever of the two is presently missing. Curtains soften the look but may be difficult to open and close; blinds let you easily control the light and bring privacy. Myriad styles of both are readily available.

> **"I use window treatments when privacy is an issue. I'll often use a vintage fabric. In my daughter's room, I use tea towels to cover the windows, and also a New Jersey State handkerchief that works as a tiny curtain."**
>
> Marie Moss, author and co-owner of M&B Vintage

54

Loop fabric over a rod. Wrap fabric in softly draped loops over a rod that's been mounted with attractive finials. Depending upon the window's width, you might have one, two, or more loops. Hem both ends. Short, they're country rustic; long, they're elegant and glamorous. Look for hardware in sewing centers that helps to position the fabric in a softly flowing fashion. Use string to test the effect so you can figure the length of fabric needed.

55

Make non-curtain curtains.

Put one or more of the vintage linen dish or
tea towels you collect on a curtain rod at the
window over the sink. Or cut strips of fabric
into different lengths and tie to a rod—they're
beautiful when they flutter in the breeze. Or try
wide, sheer ribbons decorated with seashells or
other fun, lightweight items at the ends—knot
the middle of each around a rod.

CONVERTING TABLECLOTHS

✳ **Repurpose old tablecloths** with great borders or medallions.

✳ **Cut into panels that suit your window,** and hem the sides and ends if necessary.

✳ **Create a casing to slide onto the rod,** or make them tie-tops.

✳ **Use lace for a young girl's room,** and "age" it by soaking it in tea, gently swirling the water for an even distribution of tint

✳ **1950s-style cotton tablecloths patterned with fruit** are fun for the kitchen.

✳ **Save time and effort** by attaching with theme-appropriate office clips—the kind with molded fruit, shells, or bouquets of flowers.

56

Spiff up the shades. Add color and texture to a purchased Roman or honeycomb shade by hanging a scarf or table topper over it. Fold the scarf into a triangle and tuck behind the rod. Whether the same color or contrasting, patterned or solid, this is a great way to change the décor in just a few minutes.

57
Replace curtain rods.

Rather than a standard curtain rod, use coat hooks fastened to the wall every 6 to 8 inches; you can add elegance to long curtains by tying ribbons (real, or streamers cut from the same fabric) in varying lengths from the hooks. Use curtains with grommets or tabs at the top instead of a casing. Alternatively, go for an unusual, and free, sturdy tree branch. Be sure it's wide enough for the window, and continue the outdoorsy theme by suspending the branch from plant hooks attached to the ceiling or the window frame. Use tie-on curtains.

58

Fool the eye. If windows are extremely narrow, make them look wider by hanging floor-length curtains on a rod that is wide enough to allow the curtains to be pulled completely off the window, exposing the molding. This also allows more light to enter the room. Likewise, you can make windows appear taller by installing the rods closer to the ceiling.

59

Trim your curtains. Doll up long curtains by adding pom-pom or tassel fringe to the inner and outer edges, or sew grosgrain ribbon or velvet bands along the edges and hem.

60

Gussy up curtain rods. If the rod is hidden

by the casing at the top of the curtain, a simple change of its
finials, or decorative ends, can make a big difference. Or for fun,
tie fresh or dried greens, wonderful key tassels, or even a favorite
collectible to each end of the rod.

61
Keep the curtains, change the look.

Give long, floor-to-ceiling draperies a new look by gathering panels with interesting holdbacks. Mount the holdbacks high for an elegant long and narrow window, in the middle for maximum light, or low for a traditional look. You could also bring drapery panels together in the center of the window and tie loosely with a big bow; add sparkle with glass fruit or costume jewelry bits for extra dazzle.

62

Bring shutters inside. For a down-home feel, replace curtains or blinds with louvered shutters. Prop tall ones against the wall on either side of a wide window or, for a small window, affix appropriately proportioned small ones to the wall. If you want to actually open and close them, attach with hinges.

CHAPTER SIX

PERSONALITY PLUS

✳

*Accessories That Will Turn Any House
into Your Home*

The accessories you choose and the way you arrange them
make your decor look finished and inviting and reflect your
individual taste. Pillows, wall decoration, lampshades,
door and cabinet hardware, decorative textiles
and table settings—these finishing touches are
fun to select and easy to update, embellish, or rearrange.

63
Hang objects from the ceiling.

As good as a coat of paint and easier to remove if you tire of them, natural things like dried gourds and flowers can be used to decorate the ceiling; of course, so can pretty collectibles like china cups and small pitchers. Attach ribbons or invisible wires to the items; then suspend them from pushpins, nails, or hooks in the ceiling, depending upon their weight. For a truly amazing effect in small spaces like bathrooms, cover the entire ceiling.

64

Bring nature inside. Try a garden birdbath as a decorative corner filler or hallway prop. Fill it with water and float real flower blossoms or flower-shaped candles. Another great indoor-outdoor item is an antique garden gate. Cleaned and mounted from the ceiling above a kitchen island, equipped with metal hanging hooks, it stores and displays even the most ordinary pots and pans with panache. Birdhouses and birdcages, too—from tiny wooden ones found in country markets to elaborate designs from the Victorian era—are wonderful as is or filled with potted plants. For the bedroom, try a wood or wicker plant stand at the foot of the bed.

65

Show off rugs in non-traditional ways.

No need to hide pretty rugs just because you don't have the floor space for them. Try draping a rug over a stair railing. Or hang one like a tapestry on a wall. Consider placing a rug at the head of a bed that doesn't have a headboard. Just hang it from a rod with clips or create a casing for it and attach in the back.

66

Perk up pillows. Add your own trimmings, vintage or new, to antique or store-bought pillows for an updated and personal touch. Bead shops are a great resource for shells, feathers, sequins, rhinestones, fabric leaves, and mini-tassels, among hundreds of other things from which to choose. A collection of buttons can be put to good use to button the backs, create a design or your initials, or, if you have enough of them, to edge the pillow all around. Take this idea a step further and trim sofa throws, too.

67
Change the hardware.

Exchange doorknobs, doorplates, escutcheons, doorstops, and hinges— anything that shows—for a new look in minutes. You can find old ones at antique shops and salvage stores, and brand-new reproductions with the look and feel of the past. Be sure all of the parts are included (and in good condition if the hardware is old) and will fit the door you have in mind before purchasing.

68

Dress up the fireplace.

Couldn't resist buying one more beautifully detailed iron gate, but don't have a clue what to do with it? If it is wide enough, it can be used as a fireplace screen: Lean it against the opening, or if there are children in the house, secure it so that it cannot topple over if accidentally pushed. If it is too small to act as a screen, lean it against the back wall inside the fireplace.

69

Luxe up lampshades. A hot-glue gun and a bunch of embellishments can turn any lampshade into a work of art—decorate with feathers, ribbons, shells, buttons, crystals, silk flowers, fringe applied in a pattern or hung from the top or bottom rim. Or simply paint an opaque, white paper shade a gorgeous color: Apply two or three coats of a high-gloss, oil-based paint to the outside of the shade, letting it dry between applications. Complete the transformation by gluing ribbon around the top and bottom edges, joining the ends at the shade's seam.

70

Monogram it. Iron-on embroidered letters offer an easy way to get the look, without the cost, of monogramming. Try them on lampshades, pillowcases, dining-chair slipcovers, and sofa pillows. Look for fonts that suit your style, be it curly, block, or traditional, and the piece you're embellishing.

> **"You can have the most beautiful furniture in the world, but if you forget the accessories, it's like wearing a Chanel suit with slippers."**
>
> Lee Kirch, founder of The Golden Bear, Inc.

71

Brilliant idea. Add a twinkle to your table settings with napkin rings made from sparkly buckles threaded on ribbon. Look for belt buckles and similar accessories such as vintage shoe ornaments or sweater clips at flea markets. Sew them onto the ribbon if they're not meant to be threaded. Other material options you may come across: mother-of-pearl, Bakelite, glass, or wood.

72

Change the centerpiece.

It's easy to welcome a new season by placing something different on the dining table. More provocative than a large bouquet, and sometimes easier to pull together, are fruits and vegetables: Try piling oranges and apples in a bowl; lining up lemons directly on the table or in a long, narrow container; composing red and green lettuces in beer glasses; or displaying artichokes and pomegranates in a basket. Or march a parade of plain glasses down the table center, putting a few long-stemmed posies in each.

73

Screen door frame-up.

Turn a closet into a display cabinet by replacing the door with a decorative screen door painted a brilliant color. Use the space as a fun pantry or for crafts materials storage, or display a collection of dolls, stuffed animals, or colorful crockery.

74

Re-cover old pillows.

Look around the house for discarded items to use: baby blankets, dresses, sheets, scarves, shawls, and tablecloths. To cover a bolster, simply wrap it with a length of fabric, tie the fabric together at the ends with a corded tassel or ribbon, and then fluff out the ends. Cover square pillows with a case made from two larger squares of fabric, or simply tie the squares together at each corner. Toss your new pillows on chairs and sofas, or secure them to dining chairs with ties made of the leftover fabric.

75

Skirt sinks and tables. Hide the makeshift
storage under sinks and or bedside tables by dressing them in
skirts. Think about such offbeat fabrics as lace or tulle—perhaps
from a dancer's dress found online—or use a vintage tablecloth
with a retro print. Measure the size needed, make hems, and
attach with Velcro strips or, for wood, upholstery tacks.

76

Dazzle the doors. Emphasize your home's
history or add a decorative element to a room by gluing
resin relief embellishments onto plain doors. Make it
easy on yourself by removing the doors and laying
them on the floor before setting to work. If you do keep
them hinged on the frame, temporarily support the
embellishments with tape while the glue dries. Once
the glue is completely dried, paint the entire door a solid
color for a timeless, classic look, or highlight specific
elements in a contrasting color for a more dramatic
statement.

77

Turn a frame into an organizer.

Show off favorite photos and small mementoes on an upholstered board that complements your décor: Cover a piece of fiberboard or foam core with fabric (wrap to the back for neat edges) and then arrange ribbon in a diagonal grid over the surface, gluing at the edges and securing at each intersection with a pretty upholstery brad or thumbtack. Hang the board and slip your treasures into the grid.

78

Lampshade dress-up.

Camouflage an everyday lampshade with a pretty slipcover: To make a pattern, pin a small piece of scrap fabric to one section of the shade and cut it to follow the frame contour; transfer the shape to paper and add seam allowance all around. Cut the required sections; sew together, and finish at the top and bottom with a ruffle made of the same or contrasting fabric, or lace.

79

Accessorize the accessories.

When hanging mirrors, plates, or items of any kind, singly or en masse, think about ways to enhance their visual appeal. A seductive touch for an old-fashioned mirror or a sweet painting is a swath of patterned fabric draped from a hook above, puffed to conceal the real or imaginary supporting wire, and topped with a ribbon.

ALTER
THE LIGHTING

* **Focus new attention on pieces of furniture and art** by adding lights.

* **Try lamps of varying heights** in different places to see what works best.

* **Control the ambiance and add dimmers;** they are easy to install, provide an instant mood change for any room, and will help you save electricity.

80
Spice up kitchen cabinets.

Cabinet door and drawer knobs and handles are available in an almost unlimited number of materials and styles. Before shopping, measure what you already have to ensure that replacements will fit. If the ones you want are too pricey, consider installing them only on the most visible cabinets and putting less expensive versions elsewhere. Mixing like this will work if the finish, shape, or color of the different pieces is in some way complementary, and it can actually look as good as, and more personal, than a matched set.

81

Style the kitchen sink.

Spring for an elegant faucet to create a focal point that compensates for a Plain Jane sink. Complete the makeover by putting dishwashing liquid into a piece of art glass or another pretty container, and arranging vegetable-scrubbing brush, hand soap, and sponges in a big shell or souvenir ceramic bowl.

82

Make a retro shower curtain.

Repurpose a new or vintage chenille bedspread to give
your bathroom some retro style. Hem all four sides if
you cut the spread, then make tailored tabs of the same
fabric (or use ribbon); sew or button the ends onto the
curtain, then tie or loop over the rod. You could also use
grommets or make buttonhole openings and then hang
the curtain with metal rings.

83

Make a doorstop. If you don't have an antique iron, an intriguing rock, or a small but heavy piece of sculpture, cover a brick. Wrap it with heavy fabric, folding the ends as if you were wrapping a gift, and glue or sew the edges together on the bottom.

84

Add spa-like touches to the bath.

Tie a nosegay of fresh lavender leaves and blossoms from the showerhead—the air will be filled with their delicious scent. Roll towels and washcloths and place in a large basket or copper firewood tub for easy access. Fill an old watering can with posies and perch it on the floor near the tub or on the vanity table. Upgrade to an 8" diameter showerhead that shoots out water like a refreshing rainstorm. Place eye-catching items on the windowsill or lean them on the tub's back ledge against the wall: art (framed to withstand moisture), shells, and votive candles can look romantic, playful, or elegant. Group mirrors on the wall. Replace light fixtures or lampshades—glass ones come in many shapes and finishes, not to mention the hundreds of fabric ones—and install handsome towel and robe hooks to turn this room into your favorite place to linger.

CHAPTER SEVEN

O N
D I S P L A Y

✳

*Collections
to Catch the Eye*

Here's where passion and purpose come together—
collect things you love, display them with flair,
and let your home glow with objects of interest and beauty.

85

Put ordinary things in extraordinary containers.

Everyday items like pencils and pens, makeup brushes, and dishwashing liquid look better and are more fun to use when kept in containers that have meaning for us. Use pitchers, vases, decanters, ashtrays, and baskets—you can even use dollhouses. Hung on the wall or placed on shelves and counters, these become special collections while keeping everything tidy, and they're a good way to use items the family has outgrown or no longer uses, as well as souvenirs bought when traveling.

> **"There is possibility in everything. Treasures are in your midst."**
>
> —Kathleen Hackett, co-author,
> *The Salvage Sisters' Guide*

86

Look high, look low. No matter what your collection is—plates, antique dolls, toy trains, pieces of driftwood, rocks, shells, turn-of-the-century farm tools, street signs—there is a wonderful place in your home to display it. Try the shelves above doors often found in older houses, a child's red wagon or doll carriage, or a non-working fireplace. Hang things from an old ladder affixed to the wall horizontally or propped against the wall at an angle, or on the steps of one that is open and upright. Victorian plant stands and tea carts, ordinary coat trees, on the stairs alongside the wall, and odd chairs are other possible locations.

87
Lean things against walls.

A very fashionable way to display art and large mirrors, leaning allows you to change the pieces you exhibit as often as you like without hammering a single nail.

88

The more the merrier.

The simplest items will look unique and add a personal touch to any décor if there are enough of them. Try mounting a collection of framed mirrors over a sofa or dining room buffet. Quilts piled in an armoire with the door left open to show them off radiate warmth and friendship. Copper saucepans found at yard sales and hanging in the kitchen can make for an inviting gathering spot. Glass jars used as vases lined up on the dining table add an artsy touch.

89

Make a mini-museum.

Arrange lots of small collections in a modular
shelving unit to make a wall of curiosities. Mix
in some books on the areas you collect if you like.
Balance your arrangement, keeping an eye on
color, proportion, and complexity in each unit
and overall.

"One is the loneliest number."

Barbara Siegel, collector

90

Turn anything into a collection.

All it takes is several of something that you like, each selected perhaps for its shape, color, or history. Try different arrangements in various rooms of the house. Not only ornamental, collections can camouflage architectural shortcomings, mask walls in poor condition, or fill a space while you look or save for the perfect chest or table that will someday claim it. Some collections are space-savers, too, perfect for holding important papers, holiday decorations, blankets, and other items not needed on a daily basis.

91

Show off collections in unusual ways. Display bracelets and necklaces on the branches of a coat tree. Arrange figurines among flowers and candles for a centerpiece. Cover pillows with antique textiles. Use flea-market bottles and dishes for hand soap, gel, and shampoo in the bathroom. Drape small knickknack shelves with vintage tea towels or hankies.

COLLECTORS' COUNSEL

* Group similar objects

* Have at least one unifying element—color, shape, material

* Create a focal point

* Let the color of the pieces guide your decorating scheme

* Find interesting ways to display and use the items in the collection

92

Don't forget the kitchen.

A display of run-of-the-mill cooking utensils that you use everyday can add as much interest as new wallpaper or paint. Hang colanders, spoons, skillets, and such on the wall—juxtapose shapes and materials in whatever way pleases your eye.

93

Cheap is chic. A not-so-special set of picture frames
will take on a new perspective when painted the same color.
No need for "real" art inside each. Simply decide upon a theme—
dried flowers, your collection of antique hankies or Victorian
calling cards perhaps—and fill each frame with one or more
examples. You can switch in new "art" whenever the mood hits,
or when you find a trove of something new and wonderful at
the flea market.

94

Make an art of your bookshelves.

Arrange some of the books in traditional, vertical rows and intersperse with framed paintings, photos, and works of art. Place other books in pyramidal, horizontal groups and use the resulting stacks to support clocks, paperweights, and small vases of flowers.

95

Focus on frames. Paint an assortment of
wooden frames white and hang them as a group—large
and small, plain and fancy styles—on a colored wall for
a graphic effect. Another option would be to paint
frames in a color and arrange them on a white wall, or
arrange a collection of gold frames on a deep blue, red,
or green wall. And don't worry if they're a bit rickety.
A well-driven brad or 8-penny nail can work magic.

96

Display items on easels.

Made of wrought iron, wood, or bamboo, and in sizes to hold everything from a 4-inch square watercolor to a heavy family Bible, easels have been used in the home for centuries. They are especially suited to display old sheet music, books, and magazines, as well as paintings, and are excellent when wall space is limited.

97

Background matters. If you display collectibles in a glass-door cabinet, set them off against wallpaper or fabric applied to the interior back surface of the cabinet. Choose a pattern that complements the contents as well as the cabinet style and your décor.

98

Frame fabric remnants.

Search discount bins for high-quality pieces at low prices with an eye toward those worthy of framing. To create harmony, collect textiles with a theme such as flowers, plaids, or animal prints. Vary frame sizes and styles for added interest, or paint plain wooden frames the same color for a cohesive look. Stretch and then tack the fabric to the frame backs; arrange as you would any artwork.

99

Overhead order.
Make a rustic pot rack from an old ladder—the kind with dowel rungs, not flat steps. Install eye bolts on the rails, affix sturdy chain to the eyes with S-hooks, and suspend securely from the ceiling. Use more bolts and S-hooks to hold the pans. Like any pot rack, this is a weighty accessory, so be sure to install it properly.

100

Add *pow* with presentation.

Place one item or an entire collection in front of
a mirror, perhaps on the fireplace mantel or atop
a bureau, and see how they immediately look more
significant. Line the interior of an old glass-door
cabinet or armoire with mirror or metallic paper
before arranging a collection. Place dark objects
against a white wall, and light ones against a dark
or vividly painted one. Mirrored trays from the 1930s
and '40s are also good places to gather collections
for maximum impact.

101

Use ribbons. Even ordinary plates and paintings look special when hung with ribbons rather than wires or put directly on the wall. If wires are necessary, wind a ribbon around to cover them; hide nails by gluing on something pretty like a rhinestone earring, silk flower, or interesting, oversize button.

Photo Credits

Index